Ettore Camesasca

MANTEGNA

Summerfield Press
Distributed by Frederick Muller

Contents

ISBN 0-935748-11-3 USA Pbk.
ISBN 0-584-95001-2 UK   Pbk.

© Copyright 1981 by Scala,
Istituto Fotografico Editoriale, Firenze

Photographs in black and white on pages 4,5,8
by Fratelli Alinari, Firenze

All colour photographs were taken by Scala
Photographers Angelo Corsini, Mario Falsini,
and Mauro Sarri except those reproduced on
the following pages, kindly supplied by:
13: Kunst-Dias Blauel, Gauting bei München
18,19,77,78-79: The National Gallery, London
21: Staatliche Museen, Berlin
50: The National Gallery of Art, Washington
53: Statens Museum, Copenhagen
57-64: Courtesy of H.M. The Queen of England
67: Petit Palais, Paris

English translation: Patrick Creagh

Design: Germano Facetti

Printed and bound in Italy by
Cooperativa Officine Grafiche Firenze, 1981.

Youth

Andrea Mantegna was born in 1430 or 1431, probably at Isola di Carturo, near Piazzuola sul Brenta, which was at that time under the jurisdiction of Vicenza, although it is now attached to Padua. It is in fact half-way between these two cities, and it was in Padua that the artist spent his youth.

His date of birth has been deduced from an inscription on a lost painting of 1448, in which the artist declared that he was then seventeen years old. We are therefore concerned with an exceptionally precocious talent, even in an age that abounded in precocity. The son of a carpenter, the boy was about ten years old when in 1442 he was discovered and adopted by Francesco Squarcione, who brought him up and taught him to paint. Andrea broke away from his master after a stormy lawsuit over the terms of his adoption in January 1448. It was in the same year, (on 16 May 1448), that the seventeen year-old, amongst others, was commissioned to fresco the chapel of the Ovetari family in the church of the Eremitani in Padua. As further proof of his precocity, he was chosen to join a panel of experts to assess the value of some paintings in Padua (September 15th) — he and his old master Squarcione taking opposing views in the judgement.

This adoptive father of his deserves some attention. Early historians of art made him out to be a strange figure: in part an unscrupulous and opportunist talent-scout whose brilliant adopted sons (Crivelli, Marco Zoppo etc., as well as Mantegna) sooner or later rebelled against his exploitation; and in part a crazy tailor who became a painter and collector of antique statues and copies of classical sculptures, on which it seems the prestige of his workshop was based. His only known painting, the altarpiece dated 1449 in the Padua museum, is executed in a harsh, expressive style which, in its idiosyncratic way, mixes Gothic elements with the 'new' art of Donatello.

This amalgamation of styles was at that date typical of the figurative arts in Padua where, after a long Gothic period, the Renaissance style was in-troduced initially on the arrival of Filippo Lippi in 1434, and more significantly after that of Donatello in 1443, who for ten years worked at the Basilica del Santo. The presence in neighbouring Venice of Paolo Uccello from 1423-31, and Andrea del Castagno in 1422, also had some influence on Paduan art; in 1445 Uccello was in Padua working on the fresco decoration of the Casa Vitaliani, which has since been destroyed.

These Florentines, and particularly Donatello, provided the sources for Squarcione's style, although he did not abandon the nervous line and spatial abstraction typical of Gothic painting. Even Nicolò Pizzolo, the assistant of Lippi and later of Donatello and from 1448 onwards Mantegna's associate in the Ovetari Chapel, developed on similar lines, although he grasped the implications of the Tuscan innovations more fully than Squarcione; and the same combination of traditional Gothicisms and Florentine innovation is apparent in Mantegna's own early style.

The contract for the Ovetari Chapel entrusted half of the frescoes to Mantegna and Pizzolo, and the other half to Antonio Vivarini and Giovanni d'Alemagna, two of the foremost painters in Venice. Critics have disagreed about the chronology of the various parts of the cycle, and inevitably the almost total destruction of the work during the bombing of 1944 has seriously complicated any discussion of the matter.

Assuming that the decoration began at the top of the chapel, Mantegna's earliest work in the Eremitani, which we know was completed during 1450, must be the three standing saints, Peter, Paul and Christopher, in the vault of the apse, and the *Calling of Saints James and John* and the *Preaching of St James* in the lunette at the top of the left hand wall. The style, as might be expected, is close to that of Pizzolo; there is an identical method of creating depth within the scenes, using the perspective made popular by Brunelleschi and creating a real sense of space through the laws of geometry — although without the illusionistic vistas which Donatello was able to create in his bas-reliefs at the Basilica del Santo.

In the two frescoes immediately below, *St James Baptizing Hermogenes* and *St James before Herod Agrippa*, which were executed in the following year, space seems to have been conceived in a more theatrical spirit: the point of view has been slightly lowered beneath the centre of each composition, and the vanishing point has been placed on the line separating the two scenes, so as to be common to both. In addition the *mise-en-scène* achieves a profound, almost measurable depth, and the figures are realized fully in the round by means of sharp modelling that is more typical of sculpture than of painting. The background contains a variety of details drawn from classical antiquity: pillars, medallions and marble reliefs, either sculpted with portrait busts or carved with Latin inscriptions, while in the *St James before Herod Agrippa* a triumphal arch fills two thirds of the scene. These architectural backdrops overshadow the figures, and little can be added to what has been written about them, for they have inevitably been described as the result of archaeological study, and defined as solemn, mighty, massive, compact, unshakeable and logical, heroic and classical, as well (of course) as Aristotelian. But they have been admired for different qualities too: since they radically distort the rules of classical architecture, they have earned such epithets as romantic, naive, Gothic, Shakespearean, nostalgic, even sorrowful.

Certainly, Mantegna was fascinated by antiquity. Antique pieces and copies in Squarcione's collection encouraged a taste for the classical that was to last the artist's lifetime. Even so, to emphasize this taste for the antique to the detriment of his other original qualities, as has been done, is historically inaccurate, for Jacopo Bellini, the father of Giovanni and future father-in-law of Mantegna, had already completed at least one of the famous books of drawings in which similar classical arches, capitals, friezes and medallions frame such subjects as the *Ecce Homo*, the *Flagellation* and other episodes from the Gospels, and indeed Bellini had almost certainly used some of these designs for frescoes on the walls of some church or other.

St Christopher, St Paul and St Peter
1449-50
Ovetari Chapel, Church of the Eremitani, Padua.
Photographs taken before the disastrous bombing of 1944.

Frescoes on the left wall of the Ovetari Chapel photographed before 1944.

From above:

Calling of Saints James and John, 1450; Preaching of St James, 1450.

St James Baptizing Hermogenes, 1451; St James before Herod Agrippa, 1451.

St James healing the Cripple, after 1453; Martyrdom of St James, 1453-57.

Even if Mantegna were to be credited with the first use of such antique motifs they should not be regarded as essential to the true poetry of his art. At most, this classicism forms its external aspect, and reflects a tendency widespread in the late Gothic period, when ancient ruins were seen as the fragments of a past grandeur and regarded as some kind of animating force.

The *Martyrdom of St James* was painted in 1453 by Mantegna, to complete Pizzolo's share of the work (he had been killed in a brawl). Giovanni d'Alemagna had died three years earlier, and the other survivor of the team, Vivarini, had abandoned the job in the Eremitani where, amongst other things, he still had to paint the lower part of the wall opposite that of his younger colleagues. This area, depicting the *Martyrdom of St Christopher* and the *Removal of the Body of St Christopher*, was finally painted by Mantegna; but its precarious condition (which caused it to be removed from the wall in 1865, and thus to escape the later bombing) prevents us from making an adequate analysis of it.

This has also given rise to many contrasting hypotheses as to its date: for some it was painted in 1451 or shortly after, chiefly on account of the archaic quality of the figure of St Christopher, whom the soldiers are vainly trying to shoot with arrows; for others it came later than the *Assumption of the Virgin*, and even later than the polyptych of San Zeno in Verona, which can with certainty be dated 1457-59. It would be a reasonable compromise to suppose that the two scenes of St Christopher were painted immediately before the Verona altarpiece.

Roberto Longhi has written that "the grammar of Mantegna, although intended to be classical, was in fact fundamentally anti-classical"; and it was this anti-classical quality which matured during his gradual breakaway from the late-Gothic Paduan style, as he fell under the influence of Donatello, and which is discernible in his attempt to represent the past, and the remote events of Christianity, in terms of concrete images of the present. As with the two episodes from the life of St James, those of St Christopher are seen from a single viewpoint. But whereas a gap is created between the *Baptism of Hermogenes* and *St James before Herod Agrippa* because of their different settings, in the St Christopher scenes the background is unified. In addition, the projecting pilasters framing the St Christopher

*Martyrdom of St James,
after restoration at the end
of World War II.*

Martyrdom and Removal of the Body of St Christopher
c 1452-56

From above:

Copy, painted shortly after the original, now in Paris at the Jacquemart-André Museum.

The fresco in its present state.

Detail of the upper part of the Martyrdom of St Christopher.

Colossal head
1450
Ovetari Chapel.

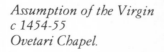

Assumption of the Virgin
c 1454-55
Ovetari Chapel.

scenes create the illusion that they are the sides of a huge window open onto the real world. Moreover, the perspective of this painted world does not draw us into its depths, but — as in all the most convincingly contrived perspectives — comes forward to meet us, making the observer part of itself as Canaletto was to do so convincingly three hundred years later.

It is probable that the growing sense of depth and plasticity in Mantegna's painting came from a very close study of Donatello's work in the Basilica del Santo. This is especially shown by his interest in

one characteristic typical of that sculptor, the framing of scenes in such a way that there is uncertainty where the pictorial space begins and the spectator's space ends. Unlike the mathematically 'correct' perspectival frames advocated by Brunelleschi, Donatello's method heightens the immediacy of the scene and the sensation of reality.

In the two Ovetari frescoes on the lower part of the wall we have already considered, the *St James Healing the Cripple* and the *Martyrdom of St James*, the lowering of the observer's point of view below the base of the frescoes was worked out by

Saints Anthony and
Bernardino holding the
Monogram of Christ
1452
Originally above the main
entrance
of the Basilica del Santo.
Padua, Museo Antoniano

Detail of Apostles at lower
left of the Assumption of
the Virgin.
Ovetari Chapel.
The Apostles not only
emerge from the frame
created by the arch,
bending backwards to see
the Virgin ascending into
heaven, but one of them
actually clings to the
outside of the scalloped
frame.

mathematical calculation, partly in relation to the
vanishing point taken for the upper scenes. But with
this new and dramatic lowering of the viewpoint
certain figures are emphasized, and by abandoning
the setting of the earlier scenes Mantegna makes a
first, if tentative, attempt to show the figures in the
scene flowing over into the space 'outside' the picture. In the *St James Healing the Cripple* the arch
leans almost dangerously out over the 'audience',
while in the *Martyrdom* the 'fourth wall' is reduced
to a fragile wooden railing on which a soldier is
leaning, with his arms 'outside' the scene.

9

Polyptych of St Luke
1453-54. 178x227 cm.
Milan, Brera.

The polyptych of St Luke (Milan, Brera), paint-ed for the church of Santa Giustina in Padua in 1453-4, is divided into many panels in the traditional Gothic form, and the figures are graded in scale according to their hierarchic importance, a typical device of the Byzantine style. These compartments have been described as a series of niches, as the gold backgrounds seem to curve: this is a result of the positioning of the individual 'statues', all seen from a single low viewpoint comparable to that of the Eremitani frescoes. And this effect must have been even more evident when the panels were still in their original frame, turning the painting into a kind of loggia, with the figures looking out, a toe or a corner of a garment projecting over the frame, while the chief subject of the polyptych, St Luke, emerges from behind his elaborate writing-desk.

Santa Eufemia
1454. 174x79 cm.
Naples, Capodimonte.
The inscription below the
Saint's feet reads 'Opus
Andreae Mantegnae---
MCCCCLIIII'.

In his easel paintings of the same date, Mantegna continued to work on the problem of convincingly portraying space and depth, at the same time intensifying the clarity and hard, gem-like solidity of his figures, the dramatic contrast between light and shade, and the plasticity of his forms. Leon Battista Alberti's precept that a 'scene' should be shown through a window was taken to its limits in the small altarpiece of *St Mark* (Frankfurt, Städelsches Kunstinstitut), dating from about 1453, and in the great *Santa Eufemia* dated 1454 (Naples, Capodimonte), which both show the protagonist framed in an arch, and highlight all projecting elements, as was by now habitual with Mantegna. The same formula is repeated in the *Saints Anthony and Bernardino holding the Monogram of Christ*, frescoed above the main entrance of the Basilica del Santo in 1452 (now in the Museo Antoniano, Padua), and in the *Assumption of the Virgin* in the Ovetari Chapel (c. 1454-55), in which the apostles not only emerge from the frame of the arch, bending backwards to see the Virgin ascending into heaven, but one of them actually clings to the outside of the scalloped frame. In this way the space created by the work of art is at one with that in which the observer stands: the barrier between reality and pictorial illusion is finally broken down, and we are admitted to share in the sacred event.

The same thing happens in the polyptych of San Zeno, deeply influenced by Donatello's altar in the Basilica del Santo, yet as a painting a complete novelty. The stage on which the sacred event takes place is set against an open-air background, analagous in concept to the two episodes of St Christopher at the Eremitani, which are themselves utterly different from the other paintings in the chapel. Even the carpet hung out of the window in the *Martyrdom of St Christopher* is similar to the one under the throne in the Verona altarpiece. The festoons suspended from the proscenium, between the simulated columns of the painting and the actual wooden ones of the frame, deliberately confuse the spectator as to what is real and what painted, and create an adventure in perspective that has nothing in common with Brunelleschi's method of projecting the image onto an ideal plane. Perspective has now become the means of achieving concrete reality.

St Mark
c 1453. 82x63,5 cm.
Frankfurt, Städelsches
Kunstinstitut.

*Polyptych of San Zeno, left
side: Saints Peter, Paul,
John the Evangelist and
Zeno
1457-59. 220x115 cm.
Verona, Church of San
Zeno*

*Polyptych of San Zeno,
centre: Madonna and Child
Enthroned with Angels
1457-59. 220x115 cm.
Verona, Church of San
Zeno.*

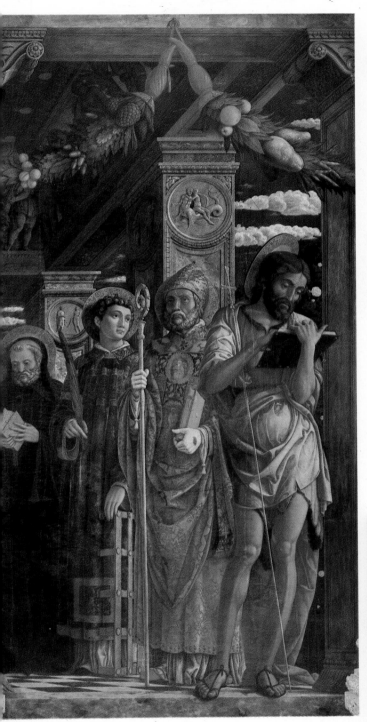

*Polyptych of San Zeno
1457-59
Verona, Church of San
Zeno
The predellas are
19th-century copies; the
original of the Crucifixion
is in the Louvre, the others
in the museum at Tours.*

*Polyptych of San Zeno,
right side: Saints Benedict,
Laurence, Gregory and
John the Baptist
1457-59. 220x115 cm.
Verona, Church of San
Zeno.*

*Detail of musician angels
from the central panel of
the polyptych of San Zeno.*

Mantegna's attempt to minimize the difference between the real and the painted world is also apparent in the predella panels of the San Zeno altarpiece (which have remained in France ever since Napoleon carried them off). These no longer depict a 'window' onto the world, but a translation of the world itself into a sacred event taking place before our eyes. The figures cut off by the frame in the foreground of the *Crucifixion* (in the Louvre) accentuate the living presence of the spectacle (as Degas was to grasp at a much later date): they are two 'extras' surprised in the act of drawing aside the veil that had concealed the mystery of life and death, rendered eternal by the intense brilliance and timeless quality of the light (Romanini, 1965).

This light is reminiscent of the atmospheric colouring of Flemish painting — works that influenced Mantegna, not only in the technique of the truncated figures, but in the expressions of grief, which may be compared for example with those of the damned in Rogier van der Weyden's *Last*

Crucifixion
67x93 cm.
Central panel of the
predella of the polyptych of
San Zeno
Paris, Louvre.

Detail of the Holy Women
from the Crucifixion.

Judgement at Beaune. If there may have been a source for this in the lost works of Piero della Francesca in Ferrara, where Mantegna spent some time in 1449, it is equally likely that he had a chance to see paintings by Rogier himself in that city, where their presence at that time is well documented, quite apart from seeing them in Venice, where Flemish paintings were also arriving at that date. In confirmation of this, the period in which Mantegna was closest to the Flemish style was during the years 1449-50, in works such as the *Adoration of the Shepherds* (New York, Metropolitan Museum), which also contain reminders of Piero, particularly in the landscape.

His friendship with Giovanni Bellini, who became his brother-in-law around 1454, may also explain the atmospheric quality of Mantegna's work at this date, and he certainly owed a debt to the Venetian for the sumptuous tones of browns, pinks and blacks, which are seen first in the altarpiece of St Luke. Indeed the *Pietà*, in the gable, has some features very typical of Bellini, though perhaps they might be equally well ascribed to the parallel development of the two artists.

As early as 1450, or shortly afterwards, the comradeship of Bellini and Mantegna is apparent in versions of the *Agony in the Garden* by both artists, who treated the subject in very different ways (both pictures are in the National Gallery, London). We have to guess at their respective roles in the genesis of these works: Mantegna probably suggested the design and layout, while the originality of the colouring is undoubtedly due to the Venetian. Mantegna's part can be deduced from the fact that Bellini's version has elements in common, not only with his brother-in-law's London painting, but also with the predella panel for the San Zeno altar of the *Agony in the Garden* (now at Tours). On the other hand, since the San Zeno altar dates from 1457-9, there is nothing to prevent us supposing that Bellini was in fact the originator of the design.

Agony in the Garden c 1455. 63x80 cm. London, National Gallery.

Judas leading the soldiers who are about to arrest Jesus. Detail from the Agony in the Garden.

The relationship between the two artists can be followed by comparing the two versions of the *Presentation in the Temple*. That in the Berlin Staatliche Museen, formerly attributed to Bellini, is now considered to be the work of Mantegna, and has been variously dated by different authorities, some believing it to be contemporary with the London *Agony in the Garden*, others dating it considerably later. It is generally thought, however, that the original conception of the composition was Bellini's, and he is believed to be the author of the almost identical picture in the Querini Stampalia Gallery in Venice. The two figures on either side of the Berlin canvas are thought to be a self-portrait of Mantegna and a portrait of Nicolosia Bellini, whom he married in 1453 or 1454. Nicolosia occupies the same position in the Venice picture, where an older woman stands beside her, perhaps her mother. On the other side, in the place of the supposed self-por-

Giovanni Bellini:
Presentation in the Temple
80x105 cm.
Venice, Querini Stampalia
Gallery.

Presentation in the Temple
c 1459-60. 67x86 cm.
Berlin, Staatliche Museen.

trait of Mantegna, there are two male figures, generally identified as Giovanni Bellini and his brother Gentile, while the old man in the centre of both pictures is usually taken to be Jacopo, father of the Bellini brothers and father-in-law of Mantegna. Thus the Berlin painting could be a votive picture for the marriage or betrothal of Andrea and Nicolosia, while the painting in Venice may be a devotional group portrait of the Bellini family.

To establish which of these paintings was made first we have to scrutinize the elements they have in common. Apart from the characterization of the priest, typical of Squarcione and a throwback to his Paduan style, it is hard not to see the hand of Mantegna in the Christ Child (although this has been denied), not only in the morphology of the face, so reminiscent of Donatello, but in the perspective that determines the child's pose, seen at an angle in relation to the back of the 'pictorial cube': by placing the child on the parapet, he gives a measure of the space behind, while at the same time 'invading' the space in front of the picture. Also the frame, interrupted in a manner typical of Mantegna, is very similar to the 'window' that he had used in the Ovetari Chapel. In the Venice canvas the window is reduced to a sill, a formula which never appeared again in Bellini's work. One must, however, recognize Bellini's personal contribution in the fluid modulation of lighting, which creates a more ample pictorial effect than was natural to Mantegna, and which he was later to put to great effect. Given the influence of Bellini still apparent in the Berlin *Presentation*, of the various dates suggested for the canvas ranging from 1454 to 1466 or even later, it seems reasonable to settle for a date just before 1460.

From Padua to Mantua

Meanwhile, in 1455, Mantegna had appealed to a Tribunal at Padua in order to obtain payment from Squarcione for the works done while in his studio. It has proved impossible to identify these works, nor do we know of any executed in collaboration with his adoptive father. In the following year Squarcione's counter-claims were rejected by the criminal courts in Venice.

It was in 1456 that Marchese Ludovico III Gonzaga, Lord of Mantua, invited Mantegna to become his court painter. The artist must have accepted almost at once, seeing that as early as 5 January 1457 the patron conveyed his satisfaction at the artist's decision to come to Mantua, but agreed that he should finish the San Zeno altarpiece before he moved. Shortly afterwards, on February 14th, a decision was made in Mantegna's favour concerning the Ovetari *Assumption* (the fresco had been questioned by the patroness who claimed that all the twelve Apostles were not visible), against the opinion of Squarcione who had been called in as an expert to testify against Mantegna.

In the end, the Marchese Gonzaga had to wait for the artist for the whole of 1458 and '59, during which time the Verona altarpiece was painted, and part of 1460. Mantegna seems to have been in Mantua from August 7th of that year, though he only took up residence there sometime before the end of November 1461.

In 1463 and 1464 the master and his assistants were working on frescoes in the Gonzaga palaces at Cavriana and Goito. Nothing remains of these cycles, nor of work done in other Gonzaga castles, since the buildings themselves were destroyed in the eighteenth century. It is just conceivable that in the engravings of the two *Bacchanals*, one including Silenus, the other with a wine cask, we have a reflection of the original decorative scheme at Cavriana, but the evidence is tenuous and could also refer to Goito. In any case these two *Bacchanal* engravings, together with the two-part engravings of the *Battle of the Sea-Gods*, constitute the best of the group of engravings attributed to Mantegna.

The problem is this: did Mantegna confine himself to supervising the reproduction of his designs as engravings, or did he practise engraving himself? From Vasari onwards (who in fact contradicts himself in the two editions of the *Lives* of 1550 and 1568), historians were inclined to regard Mantegna as the 'first engraver of prints in Italy', as Lomazzo wrote in 1584. The same writer, in 1578, even called him 'the inventor of the great art of printing', an assertion which cannot be reconciled with the acknowledged priority of the Germans, who had been making woodcuts since at least 1430.

In 1466, and again in 1467, Mantegna spent some time in Tuscany, the first time in Florence, the second in Pisa, where he painted frescoes in the Camposanto that have not come to light. It was in Tuscany that the earliest experiments in engraving in *niello* (i.e. metal engraving) were made, which Antonio del Pollaiolo adopted as a technique to reproduce his own drawings. It is impossible to be sure of the extent of Mantegna's own intervention in the making of the engravings, but the quality of the seven best works that go under his name is high enough to suggest that he may have done them himself.

As early as 4 May 1459 Ludovico Gonzaga had written to Mantegna that the chapel in the castle of San Giorgio, which was the Marchese's residence in Mantua itself, had been arranged 'in your way' — that is, according to the specifications of the artist. In 1565 Vasari saw a work of Mantegna's in this chapel which some modern scholars identify as the triptych in the Uffizi in Florence, though this is not otherwise recorded before 1587. This hypothesis is not universally accepted, and those who challenge it hold that the triptych belongs to the Florentine visit; but the lack of cohesion between its elements does lend substance to the theory that the three panels may have been executed at different times and put together later (the frame is certainly nineteenth century). In fact, apart from the completely different

Bacchanal with Silenus. 1463-64. 31x45 cm. Engraving.   *Bacchanal with Wine Cask. 1463-64. 31x44 cm. Engraving.*

Ascension, left panel of the
Uffizi triptych
c 1460. 86x43 cm.
Florence, Uffizi.

Circumcision, right panel
of the Uffizi triptych
c 1469. 86x43 cm.
Florence, Uffizi.

setting of the *Circumcision* compared to that of the *Epiphany* and *Ascension*, and the fact that the three episodes are not normally shown together, it must be said that the *Ascension* is still close in format to the Ovetari *Assumption* and that, like the *Epiphany*, it can be compared to the San Zeno altarpiece; whereas the *Circumcision* contains features that suggest it was finished in about 1470. A fourth painting, the *Death of the Virgin* (Madrid, Prado), has been cut down: originally the fragment of *Christ With the Soul of the Virgin* (private collection) formed the upper half of the painting, which was of the same size as the *Circumcision* and the *Ascension*.

Epiphany, central panel of the Uffizi triptych c 1462. 76x77 cm. Florence, Uffizi.

(left)
Detail of
the central part of the
Circumcision.

(right)
Detail of
the left side of the
Epiphany.

So, although it cannot be conclusively proved, it is probable that these four paintings, together with others since lost, formed part of a series of paintings destined for the palace chapel in Mantua, of which we have documentary evidence; it would be strange if another work of this kind had existed without any reference to it being made in documents. As for the *Ascension*, there is little to add about it that has not already been said in respect of the predella of the San Zeno altarpiece. In the *Epiphany* we should mention the great black area of the grotto, which counterbalances the gaudiness of the robes and trappings of the three kings and their suite, complete with camels. In the *Circumcision* the subtle rhythm of the figures is balanced by that of the architecture in the background. The precision and brilliance with which this is painted, however, makes the background dominate the composition, which might suggest that it was added as the result of some change of plan, or at any rate at a later date than the foreground, showing as it does features that were to become trade marks of Mantegna's workshop. The *Death of the Virgin* has been particularly singled out for praise: here reds, yellows, carmines and blues are put together with a boldness that anticipates El Greco, while the pool of light in the centre of the floor would have been an astonishing innovation even in Carpaccio's day (who was a child when Mantegna painted this panel).

Further confirmation that the 'scenic wall' of the *Circumcision* must have been a later addition comes from a comparison with the *St Sebastian* in the Louvre, generally dated in the 1470's: this is in turn related to the *St Sebastian* in Vienna (Kunsthistorisches Museum), where the splendid architecture of the Florentine painting, depicted with the same exactitude, is practically repeated, although now shown in a ruined state.

Christ with the Soul of the Virgin
1461. 27x17 cm.
Ferrara, Baldi Collection.

Sketch showing the two paintings as originally joined together in a single work.

Death of the Virgin (Dormitio Virginis) 1461. 54x42 cm. Madrid, Prado.

(left)
St Sebastian
After 1470. 68x30 cm.
Vienna, Kunsthistorisches
Museum.

(right)
St Sebastian
c 1480. 275x142 cm.
Paris, Louvre.

*Profile of a Man
1461. 33x25 cm.
Milan, Poldi Pezzoli
Museum.*

*Portrait of Cardinal Carlo
de' Medici
1466. 41x30 cm.
Florence, Uffizi.*

*Portrait of Cardinal
Francesco Gonzaga
After 1461. 25x18 cm.
Naples, Capodimonte.*

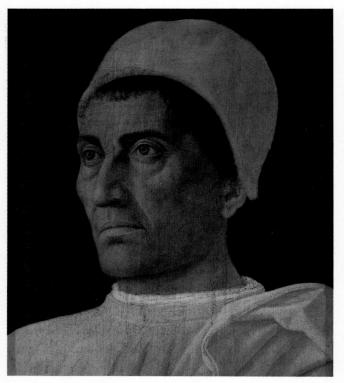

Our glance at these two St Sebastians has led us into a much later period of Mantegna's Mantuan sojourn, and we must return to his earlier years in the city. The portrait of *Cardinal Ludovico Mezza-rota*, in the Berlin Staatliche Museen, was probably painted during the Ecumenical Council of 1458-60, which took place in Mantua. With some justification this portrait has been called the pictorial equivalent of Donatello's *Gattamelata* (1446-50) with which it shares a metallic compactness of form. The portrait of *Cardinal Francesco Gonzaga* (Naples, Capo-dimonte), which dates from just after 1461, the year in which the sitter was created a cardinal, is gentler by comparison. The delicate yet punctilious brush strokes, breathing life into the sulky features of the young prelate, appear again in the *Profile of a Man* in Milan (Poldi Pezzoli), although recently scholars have questioned the autograph status of this painting. Despite the heavy studio intervention apparent in the large canvas of *St Bernardino with Angels* in the Brera, Milan, it contains similar qualities and the spectacular sense of space is preserved; it has now been established that this canvas, too, was painted in Mantua.

The Bridal Chamber
(Camera degli Sposi)

The parapet in the background of the Brera *St Bernardino with Angels* echoes the parapet on the Donatello reliefs for the High Altar in the Basilica del Santo in Padua, and it appears again behind the family group in one of the two great frescoes in the *Camera degli Sposi*, or Bridal Chamber in Mantua, as well as on the painted dado around the walls of this room.

We have now reached what, after the disappearance of his other paintings of equal magnitude, must be considered Mantegna's most important surviving work. It consists of the paintings on the walls and ceiling of a room practically cubic in form (the sides each measuring about 8.05 metres) in the north tower of the Castel San Giorgio in Mantua. The Chamber may originally have been a bedroom, but it very soon came to serve as a small ceremonial chamber, and after the death of the Marchese Ludovico, who commissioned the frescoes, appears to have become a storeroom for precious objects. The damage done by the siege of 1630, when Imperial troops occupied the castle, was worsened by the neglect of the Austrian authorities, though it is to them that we owe the first (clumsy) attempts at restoration. The silence that reigned amongst critics for much of the nineteenth century is reflected by M. Armengaud in his *Galeries publiques de l'Europe* (Paris, 1862-65), where, under Mantua, the Palazzo del Te is mentioned but there is not a word about the castle or about Mantegna ('In Mantua an Austrian sentry guards the museums...') The Bridal Chamber, in particular, was degraded to the status of a store for notaries' records, and as such it remained until 1880. Another thirty-five years were to pass until, in 1915, it reacquired the status of a work of art.

The decoration includes the ceiling, in the centre of which is the famous *trompe-l'oeil*, painted as if the room were open to the sky, and the *sotto-in-sù* balustrade (i.e. shown in extreme illusionistic perspective) over which women look down, while putti play, a vase balances precariously and a peacock perches. The whole *tromp-l'oeil* effect is enclosed in a circular garland, which is in turn contained in a square stucco frame, to which are attached eight caissons, or lozenge shapes; these again frame twelve triangular sections. The frames of these sections, the medallions within the lozenge shapes which enclose portrait busts of Roman emperors, and the mythological episodes in the triangular sections, are painted in grisaille, in imitation of marble reliefs on a gold mosaic ground. The frames converge on the corbels placed above pilasters which are simulated in paint on the walls. Each wall is divided by the pilasters into three arched bays, and around the base of the room runs a dado, also painted. In the twelve lunettes above the frescoed scenes are depicted festoons bearing the emblems of the Gonzaga family. On the level of the corbels which, together with the cornices over the doors and the fireplace, are the only carved stone elements in the room, there are painted curtain rails between one pilaster and another, supporting leather curtains stamped with gold designs and lined with blue. On two of the walls the curtains are lowered, and we know that on special occasions they were covered by real leather curtains of identical design, perhaps from Cordoba; these were considered to be amongst the most precious objects in the Gonzaga collection.

On the two other walls the curtains are drawn back so as to show two scenes: that of the *Court* includes the Marchese Ludovico, his wife Barbara of Brandenburg, their children, relations and courtiers; the other depicts the *Meeting* between Ludovico Gonzaga and his son Cardinal Francesco (who has grown so stout that one can scarcely recognize the slender youth in the Naples portrait), together with various persons in their suites; behind them stretches a landscape with hills and citrus trees, while grooms, horses and dogs wait some way off.

The decorations turn the room into a kind of open-air pavilion, and the cunning use of painted architectural elements creates the illusion of a high vault, though in fact the real vault is comparatively

The ceiling with the trompe-l'oeil *of the Camera degli Sposi (Bridal Chamber). Mantua, Ducal Palace.*

Detail of two women and a putto from the trompe-l'oeil *ceiling. Camera degli Sposi.*

low. As in the Pantheon in Rome, a building which was a source of inspiration for Renaissance artists, Mantegna has created an opening to the sky. Although the *Meeting* is intended to look as if it is set just outside the imaginary pavilion, the scene of the *Court* is apparently taking place on a terrace jutting into it, enclosed at the back by a parapet in the style of Donatello, and extending on the right to a short flight of steps. Descending these steps into an anteroom, the view is partially blocked by yet another curtain through which we glimpse a sunny courtyard with builders at work. It is a spectacular conception even now, and must have been irresistible before it was spoilt by deterioration and clumsy restoration.

Yet when we attempt to decipher the actual theme of all this, we are justified in feeling a certain measure of uncertainty. Obviously, the *Meeting* shows Ludovico III greeting his son, who was created cardinal in 1461. But history records two such

meetings, each worthy of being immortalized in paint, and it is unclear if this is the meeting which took place immediately after Francesco took the purple, or that of 1472, when he returned to Mantua to assume the titular cardinalship of Sant'Andrea. In the first case the prelate came from Milan, in the second from Bologna. Just to confuse the issue, the city in the background is Rome: a very idealized Rome, shown in all its imperial grandeur, probably the invention of a fifteenth century humanist who had never been there. Certain landmarks are recognizable: the Colosseum, the pyramid of Caius Cestius, the Theatre of Marcellus and the Ponte Nomentano. But perhaps Rome is here intended, after all, as a symbol of the Church, to augur well for the cardinal's future career.

If we bear in mind that the cardinal's hat brought the Gonzaga dynasty more glory than any previous honour, it seems logical to connect the court scene with this event as well; though here there are even greater uncertainties. Given the significance that was attached to such paintings at that time, it seems unlikely that the *Court* is simply a group portrait. Less than a hundred years later, painting a family group like this could merely have been a device to create a 'lively and spontaneous' pose — as every amateur photographer knows today. But in the fifteenth century no painted event was ever without significance, and in this Mantuan court scene it is evident that something is taking place on the left of the picture: the Marchese, who holds a letter in his hand, is speaking to someone, probably a secretary, while on the other side there is a commotion, perhaps heralding an arrival.

This is not idle speculation for if we could understand Mantegna's theme we might be able to date the painting and evaluate its position in his work, thereby partly overcoming the disadvantages of bad restoration and other damage (as early as 1630 the Landsknechts fired pistol shots into the room, and damp, flooding and continual condensation have done the rest). That the frescoes have been variously dated between 1465 and 1490-91 shows the necessity for further study.

We do however have a firm date in the dedicatory inscription in the centre of the wall showing the *Meeting*. It is in poor condition, especially at the bottom where the date is painted, but it does at least imply that the work was finished in 1474. There is additional confirmation of this in two letters of 17 and 23 March 1474, ordering 'two *migliara* of beaten gold' and then 'another two', and a 'pound of good German blue' for 'our chamber in the castle'. Now these were materials, gold leaf and blue made of lapis lazuli, that on account of their high cost were applied to wall paintings at the end of the

Detail from the ceiling with two of the eight Roman Emperors. Camera degli Sposi.

Detail of one of the lunettes on the north wall above the scene of the Court. Camera degli Sposi.

work, so that they should not be wasted. In additon, in the very next year the government of Mantua issued an act drawn up in the 'camera magna picta' of Castel San Giorgio, which for various reasons may be identified with the *Camera degli Sposi*.

And when did work begin? Some critics, calculating that the number of square metres painted corresponds to two years' work, and subtracting that from 1474, have settled for 1472 or 1473. In an essay of 1964 the present writer preferred to base his calculations on formal and technical evidence. This takes us back to the year scratched, probably by Mantegna himself, on a corner of the window between the two painted scenes: *'1465 . d . 16 . iunii'*, that is, 16 June 1465. Later, the discovery by

Migliorini (1972) of other letters of the Marchese confirmed this deduction. In one, dated 26 April 1465, he ordered two cartloads of lime 'to be used to paint our chamber in the castle', while in another of a much later date (22 October 1470) he laments the fact that 'it is many years now since he began to paint that chamber of ours, and he has not yet done half'. In other words, after years of work, the job was barely half finished.

It therefore becomes probable that the event recorded in the scene of the *Meeting* is that of 1461. as we have said, the cardinal was travelling from Milan, for as soon as he received his nomination while 'in studio' at Pavia, he had gone to pay a visit to the Duke of Milan, Francesco Sforza, whose good offices had been decisive in his gaining the purple. The chronicles tell us that at that time the duke's health was bad, sinking to the point 'quaxi de morte' almost to death. In fact as soon as the new Cardinal had departed, the Duchess Bianca Maria Sforza wrote to the Marchese Gonzaga asking him to come and help her deal with the unpredictable results of her husband's imminent decease. Ludovico III was commander of the Sforza troops, and he must have

The Court, north wall.
1. Marsilio Andreasi, Ludovico III's secretary;
2. Ludovico III;
3. Gianfrancesco, Ludovico's third child;
4. Protonotary Ludovico (?);
5. Paola, youngest child of the Gonzagas (?);
6. Rodolfo, fourth son;
7. Barbara of Brandenburg;
8. Barberina (?).

been on the road at once. Let us quote the words of the chronicler Schivenoglia: "at once the Marchese mounted his horse to go to Milan, and when he was at Bozzolo he met the above-mentioned Cardinal; at a distance of a crossbow shot the Marchese, his father, dismounted and went towards him on foot, and likewise the Cardinal advanced towards his father. And when they were near each one made a great bow, and the Marchese his father spake these words, and that is: 'As in the world I wish to be your father, but as in God I wish to be your son , I prithee thank Almighty God that he has made you a fine gift, and ask you to consider it a fine gift, and a great happiness'. And thus, weeping for joy, they parted the one from the other."

The appointment to the cardinalship had been announced on 22 December 1461, while the meeting near Bozzolo — a Gonzaga stronghold about ten kilometers from Mantua — took place on January 1462.

As in Schivenoglia's account, the composition painted by Mantegna focuses on the figure of the Cardinal, placed in the centre of the composition and further heightened, as it were, by the tree behind him, while the dignified austerity of the Marchese is in perfect keeping with the solemnity with which he greets his son. But the faces of the people involved, beginning with the two main protagonists, are anachronistic: they are at least ten years older than they should be if the scene represented took place in 1461. Turning to the landscape, including the view of Rome, there is nothing wintry about it, and mountains such as these are certainly unknown around Bozzolo.

Nor, however, do they exist at Bondanello, the scene of the meeting in 1472, even if the building in the course of construction, behind the scene of the horses and grooms, may be identified as the 'grandiose palace' which from 1468 on had been under construction (by order of Ludovico) at Gonzaga, of which town Bondanello is a dependency.

Another point: in the fresco with the horse we can just make out a number of figures that have nearly disappeared because they were painted on dry intonaco. They form a procession with dromedaries, and could represent the journey of the Magi who on January lst were still on their way to Bethlehem (this was suggested by Signorini in 1972). This is an indication in favour of the meeting at Bozzolo, and underlines the symbolic character of the landscape, including the dreamlike Rome.

If, then, we accept that the episode represents the meeting of 1461, or rather 1462, we might infer that the *Court* belongs to the same period. And in fact the same critic (Signorini) has established that the message to the Marchese, with the pressing summons from the Duchess of Milan, was delivered at Castel San Giorgio on the morning of 1 January 1462. The letter, dated *'1461. 30. xbre.'* is marked 'cito cito' (urgent urgent), and is now in the Gonzaga archives in Mantua. It seems that we are justified in seeing it as already in the hands of its recipient in the *Court* scene.

It has also been pointed out that the paper in Ludovico's hand has no writing on it. But from the way it is presented the writing must be on the side we do not see, otherwise the secretary would not be able to read it. However, on the side we do see, there ought to be the address with the 'cito cito', as on the original in the Gonzaga archives.

But its position, in the middle of the sheet, is hidden by the knob of the faldstool on which the Marchese is seated. It has been deduced from this that Ludovico, and Mantegna on his behalf, wished to 'punish' the Duke of Milan for having refused, in 1463, to agree to the marriage between his heir and Dorotea, daughter of the Marchesi Gonzaga: and to do so with the most terrible punishment of all as far as posterity is concerned — silence. As if to prove it, in the *Meeting* the duchess's letter, now in the hands of the Cardinal, is blank; or rather, it contains a jumble of letters that may very likely be taken as the painter's signature: 'Andrea me pi(nxit).' These are the conclusions of Signorini's first iconographical researches (1972).

The investigation was continued by Mulazzani (1978), revealing a connection between the 'programme' of the Chamber and a passage in the Panegyricus, or eulogy, of Pliny the Younger on the Emperor Trajan. This would first of all explain the theme of the 'oculo' in the centre of the ceiling, which had previously remained obscure, particularly as regards the inclusion of the black woman. She must have been a servant, or indeed a slave. We have documentary evidence that Renaissance courts had negroes in their households for 'ornament and entertainment', who could be bought from the slave-traders in Venice and elsewhere. The great ladies of the time were very proud of them, boasting to one another of the 'negritude' of their handmaids. This happened just as much in Mantua as elsewhere.

To continue with the ceiling, scholars have been particularly struck by the features of the white woman leaning her head towards that of the black one. Without doubt there is some resemblance to the Marchesa Barbara, wife of Ludovico III, who dominates the centre of the *Court* scene, and this identification has some illustrious supporters. But to imagine a woman of such austere conduct behaving so confidentially towards a slave seemed inconceivable to others, so that certain students, the present writer included, have down-graded the white woman to the status of servant.

In the light of Pliny's Panegyricus, the two women should be understood as allegories of domestic harmony, and in particular that between masters and servants. The presence of the peacock, connected with Juno, would tend to confirm this, symbolizing harmony between spouses, as would the orange-tree, also connected with marriage. And we should remember that in the dedicatory inscription this room, which has traditionally been called the *Camera degli Sposi* (Bridal Chamber), is dedicated to 'the Most Illustrious Ludovico' and to

Marchese Ludovico Gonzaga III with his secretary Marsilio Andreasi.

'the Illustrious Barbara, his consort.'

Pliny's Panegyricus would also lead us to suppose that the theme of harmony presented on the ceiling is interwoven with that of political prestige. In this context the *putti* are a reference to glory, as are the busts of the eight Roman emperors — Julius Caesar and his seven successors down to Galba, who were at that date considered to be more glorious than the later emperors — and the episodes depicted in the lozenges. Three of these are devoted to Orpheus and five to Hercules, men who shared the glory of divinity, while the two dealing with Arion might refer to the fame he earned from his skill as a navigator and sailor, and the presence of Periander might be explained by his renowned wisdom.

As for Ludovico's reasons for likening himself to Trajan, the prototype of the just but absolute ruler, these could be explained by reference to his internal policy. In 1467 the Marchese abolished the offices of mayor, vicar and so on, in order to concentrate the government in his own hands. To the same end, seven ecclesiastical titles were transferred to Cardinal Francesco and others, but deprived of all effective power. All this, according to the chroniclers, was a cause of discontent. The 'programme' of the Chamber, therefore, or at least what can be seen of it today, would have been drawn up only after these events, as a statement of the Marchese's aims.

In the end we shall have to leave the reader to pick his own way through the various interpretations of the frescoes. He can choose one of the themes, or attempt to reconcile them all: the theme of the friendship between the Sforzas and Ludovico and Francesco Gonzaga (although there is no direct reference to the Dukes of Milan, since the address is omitted from the letter); or the theme of the celebration of domestic peace, coupled with the justification of absolute sovereignty.

What is particularly interesting, however, is the change of plan which took place when the work had already been in hand for some years (Signorini, 1972; Mulazzani, 1978), to which must be added (Mulazzani) the divergence between the strict realism of the court scene and the abstract qualities of the *Meeting* (including the idealised view of Rome, the ambivalent indications of the season, and the discrepancy in the age of the protagonists compared to the supposed date of the meeting).

At this point it is worth summarizing our 1964 'reading' of the frescoes which reached similar conclusions. On the basis of this evidence we can assume that the *Court* was painted at about the time of Mantegna's journey to Tuscany, that is in 1465 or 1466, possibly as an independent work, or at least with a decorative surround very different from what we see now. We can get some idea of the original appearance from the simulated green marble beside the window where the date 1465 has been inscribed. The *Meeting* was frescoed much later, in about 1473-74, or at any rate, after Mantegna's stay in central Italy.

According to some critics, Mantegna was open to many influences during his visits to Florence and Pisa. Piero della Francesca, Donatello, Filippo Lippi, Andrea del Castagno's Florentine work, Verrocchio's work before he moved to Venice, Baldovinetti, Pollaiolo, Botticelli and others were all carefully studied by Mantegna and had a long and lasting effect on his style.

Today this thesis has been contested, and it is denied that these two journeys had any artistic consequences for Mantegna. In fact, the influence on his style seems really to have been negligible. Little can be learnt from the portrait of a *Cardinal* in the Uffizi, possibly Carlo de' Medici and perhaps painted in Florence (although some scholars consider it to be a sixteenth century copy), or from the *St George* in the Venice Accademia, usually dated 1467 or immediately after. Indeed the only echoes of his Florentine sojourn are derived from Castagno's *Illustrious Men*, and even then not at first hand, but from the somewhat exaggerated re-interpretations of Benozzo Gozzoli. In addition to this Benozzo's landscapes in the Camposanto in Pisa and some of his Roman notebooks are perhaps the source of the classical architecture used in the view of Rome in the *Meeting*. These sketches Mantegna instilled with life, and in particular emphasized the white building above Ludovico's head, an extraordinary anticipation of a Palladian villa.

Critics dislike the idea that Mantegna owed anything to the 'gossiping' Benozzo, who was however, with some justification, fashionable at that time at the court of the Medici, who were discriminating patrons of art. But we need only compare the composition of the *Meeting* with that of Gozzoli's *Building of the Tower of Babel* (Pisa, Camposanto), which in 1467 must have been in its early stages, to understand the source of his conception: the idea of lining up the figures at the front of the scene, and placing a huge tree behind them out of which Mantegna makes so strong an image that it counterbalances the gold of the dedicatory inscription immediately beside it as well as the craggy mountains in the scene of the horses on the other side of the wall.

Barbara of Brandenburg, wife of Ludovico III. The Bridal Chamber is dedicated to 'the Most Illustrious Ludovico' and to 'the Illustrious Barbara, his consort.'

Grooms with horse and
two dogs. West wall,
Camera degli Sposi.

(right)
Dedicatory inscription.
West wall, Camera
degli Sposi.

In fact the only lasting effect of these two visits to Tuscany is to be found in Mantegna's use of cooler colours, very different from the density of colour employed in the *Court* which is, in this respect, still close to the San Zeno altarpiece when compared to the airy transparency of the *Meeting*.

Returning to the chronological gap between the painting of the two scenes, it is possible that this might be explained by a change of plan on the part of Ludovico himself; and, as might be expected from a general restructuring of the cycle, it could even explain the discrepancies apparent in the court scene. For if we take the *Court* to have formed part of a programme that was later abandoned, it is reasonable to assume that, once the second programme was established, this painting would have undergone some changes, and these probably included the idea that the scene should be set in a kind of pavilion. For example, the courtier in front of the pilaster above the fireplace was painted before the pilaster was added in behind him, so that he stands on a plane that is no longer part of the scene. The same is true of the courtier, taken to be a secretary, who leans towards the Marchese. The torso of the figure to the left of the young courtier is overlapped by a sleeve that is patently not his, and presumably belonged to a figure which disappeared when the pilaster was painted in to provide the *Court* with its new setting: in the course of an insensitive restoration an extra sleeve has been revealed, which Mantegna must have either hidden or transformed. The other courtier beside the beau, awkwardly placed beside the pilaster, makes sense only if we imagine that he is addressing a figure who has since been covered by the pilaster. The steps on the right of the fireplace are an extraordinary lapse in perspectival construction for the author of the Ovetari frescoes; and in this case too we may assume that we have lost the retouching which would have changed the angle at which they now appear.

The difference of pictorial material in the two scenes has intrigued critics for a long time. In the *Meeting* the fresco technique is evident from the chalky clarity of the colours, the manner of the brushstrokes, and above all from the joints between one day's work and the next, from which we can see that the whole scene was painted in about thirty instalments: not an exceptional number of sections for the fresco painters of the later fifteenth century, especially for Mantegna who was so extremely exact. But as we have already noted, the surface of the paint in the *Court* is dense and pasty, and the borders between one day's work and the next have

almost entirely disappeared; this proves that there was an extensive reworking 'a secco', that is, on dry plaster, and would be a natural result given the changes we have suggested.

Moreover, if we imagine the figures in the *Meeting* as three dimensional and viewed from above, we would see a diagonal arrangement which concentrates the observer's attention on the section containing the Marchese and the Cardinal. This arrangement is not present in the *Court*, where we are not confined to a single viewpoint, as we are in the double scenes in the lower part of the Ovetari chapel, and this lack of organic consistency confirms the suggestion that the fresco was worked on at different times.

It is also interesting to apply the rules of the Golden Section to the *Camera degli Sposi*. This was a system of proportions, used by classical architects, whereby a straight line is divided in such a way that the ratio of the smaller section to the larger equals that of the larger section to the whole. There is no documentary evidence that Mantegna used it in the Chamber or indeed elsewhere, but it had been in widespread use at least since the time of Giotto. The *Meeting* displays harmonious relationships between the painted elements, especially (but not only) the pilasters, simulated in paint, and the real architectural features such as the door-jambs. Evidently this was done to obscure the asymmetric placing of the actual door (which is not in the middle of the wall), and to exploit it to liven up the whole composition. In the same scene, the Golden Section proportions are also applied to the ratio between the height of the figures and the overall height of the wall. On the wall containing the *Court* only this latter system of proportion is applied. For instance the Golden Section proportions exist between the overmantle and the painted rail supporting the fake curtain; but not between the position of a corbel, for instance, and a painted vertical element. This is additional confirmation of the fact that the *Court* was laid out independently, before the idea of the pavilion structure in which they sit was conceived.

We have already noticed that the parapet behind the *Court* is derived from the art of Donatello. To have used it in 1465 would have been highly original in Mantua. It is far less likely that Mantegna would have had recourse to it seven or eight years later, that is if a later date is proposed for the court scene. The cold blue sky in the *Court* is like the sky in the Ovetari frescoes and the San Zeno polyptych, and quite unlike the sky of the *Meeting* and of the ceiling. To make it match the later work it was

overpainted in a paler shade of blue, but today much of this overpaint has fallen off and obscures the original in only a few places. Finally, while we have already pointed out the probable effects of the Tuscan journey on the *Meeting*, to find a precedent for the *Court* we have to look to Donatello's reliefs in the Basilica del Santo in Padua; and the way light gleams on those bronzes is evoked by Mantegna in the more deliberate lighting of the scene from one side only, indirectly identified with the light coming from the east window in the Chamber.

We must apologize for this lengthy examination of the *Camera degli Sposi*. It was necessary in order to reconstruct the genesis of the frescoes and to give some account of the ideas and events that shaped them and modified them in the course of time. A photograph taken before the restorationworks begun in 1876 bears witness to the vicissitudes it has suffered; it shows the room in an indescribable state of decay, but the details are probably closer to the original state than those we see today.

In conclusion, it could be said that the work is the culmination of a dialogue between artist and observer, begun around 1450 at the Eremitani church and here brought to its zenith. In the San Zeno altarpiece the observer was included in the space of the 'sacra conversazione', while now he finds himself at the centre of the space created by the painting and the roles are reversed: it is he, the observer, who is himself observed by the painted figures, by the Gonzagas; indeed he is actually spied on from above, thanks to an unprecedented piece of trickery so intriguing that it was later to become

The Meeting, west wall.
1. Ludovico III;
2. Cardinal Francesco, Ludovico's second child;
3. Francesco, first son of Federico I;
4. Sigismondo, third child of Federico I;
5. Ludovico the Protonotary, youngest son of Ludovico III;
6. Federico I, first born son of Ludovico.

widely imitated (Romanini, 1965). Bramante, passing through Mantua in 1477, may have been the first to fall under its fascination. Here perspective is no longer used to project us into the world of the painting, or to project this world towards us, but for the first time to include the observer within the painted world, so that the persons and things created by the artist's brush live through the same experience as the observer. The Gonzagas and ourselves are part of the same reality, and inhabit the same space. Mantegna has made it so that the event is not recalled or evoked, but lived through in the very instant of its taking place.

We have yet to give some indication of the identification of the figures, a problem complicated not only by the restorations, but by the impossibility of establishing the identity of various persons connected to the Gonzaga court (on coins, medals and so on) and additionally confused by traditional identifications which are not necessarily accurate or reliable. For example, the unknown person shown in profile to the right of the Marchese in the meeting scene has been variously identified as a member of the circle of Pico della Mirandola, or as Gianfrancesco the third son of the Marchese, or even as his daughter Dorotea, the bride turned down by the Sforzas.

However, to continue with the characters in the

Meeting, apart from Ludovico III Gonzaga (1414-1478) and his second son Cardinal Francesco (1444-1483), scholars are in general agreement as to the identity of his eldest son, the future Federico (1441-1484), who is the man in profile on the extreme right. Federico's son and heir, the future Francesco II (1466-1519), with the unmistakeable 'craggy brow', is the child between the Marchese and the Cardinal; the smallest child is Federico's third son Sigismondo (1469-1525), also destined to become a cardinal; and the future protonotary Ludovico (1458-1511), the youngest male child of the Marchese Ludovico, who became a bishop in 1468, is shown here giving his hand to his brother the Cardinal and to his nephew who was to become one, thus forming the ecclesiastical trio of the family. The figure in profile facing Federico Gonzaga has generally, though with some reservations, been thought to be Leon Battista Alberti, the great architect who from 1459 to 1470 worked in Mantua; but recent criticism favours its identification as Frederick III of Hapsburg, Holy Roman Emperor from 1452, who according to some early commentators is represented in the chamber (although they believed that he was in the other scene). The head next to his, also turned towards the future Frederick I, was until recently tacitly assumed to be a self-portrait, though the likeness to the funerary bust of

*St George
c 1467. 66x32 cm.
Venice, Academy.*

Mantegna in Sant'Andrea in Mantua is not very convincing; it is now thought to be that of Christian I of Denmark, who may also be represented in the cycle. As for Mantegna, himself, now that he has been excluded from the *Meeting*, his portrait has been tentatively recognized in the mask on the pilaster between the meeting scene and the dedicatory inscription, slightly above the level of the skyline.

Proceeding to the court scene, the person bending over the Marchese, and generally taken to be his secretary, or one of his secretaries, has been identified as Marsilio Andreasi, although there is no firm proof. Immediately behind Ludovico, the robust dignitary shown in a three quarter view (who in the pre-1876 photo, mentioned earlier, has harsher features almost like a Tartar) might be the Marchese's third son Gianfrancesco (1445-1496). Then we find Barbara von Hohenzollern of the Brandenburg line (1423-1481), wife of Ludovico III since 1435 (or possibly later, the date of their marriage is unknown). As for the child beside her, suggestions for her identity range from Paola, youngest child of the couple, born in 1464, to her sisters Cecilia, Barbara and Dorotea, or to Chiara (1467-1503), second child of the Marchese's heir, Federico; while some have thought it a portrait of the protonotary Ludovico. The young man behind the Marchesa could be Rodolfo (1451-1495), fourth son of the eleven (or thirteen) children of the ruling couple. The pretty girl who comes next may be the fourth from youngest child, Barbara, or Barberina (1456-1503), but there are plenty of other identifications proposed. In front of her is the famous dwarf, whom some scholars have taken to be Cecilia Gonzaga, third daughter of the couple (we do not know when she was born, though it was almost certainly after Rodolfo and before Barberina), or for her sister Paola; one illustrious Mantegna specialist (1927) referred to this figure as a 'monstrous dwarf.' The Marchesa Barbara's liking for dwarfs is evident in a number of letters, which mention a 'Beatricina de' Gatti da Pavia', a 'Maddalena' and others, although they give no biographical information. Nor can we identify the hunchback who is bustling about on the extreme left hand side of the picture. He could be a jester, or a commoner or, as some have asserted, even a Gonzaga; for Paola Malatesta, wife of Gianfrancesco (1395-1444) and mother of Ludovico III, had introduced rickets into the family, and we know that the Marchese himself and several of his children suffered from this complaint; indeed Mantegna seems to have done little to conceal the fact.

49

Madonna and Child
c 1470. 43x35 cm.
Milan, Poldi Pezzoli Museum.

The Christ Child Blessing
c 1475. 70x35 cm.
Washington, National
Gallery.

Madonna and Child
c 1470. 43x31 cm.
Bergamo, Accademia
Carrara.

A number of paintings of the Madonna and Child belong to the same period as the *Camera degli Sposi*, still showing the influence of Filippo Lippi and Donatello, and painted in thin glazes of tempera that let the grain of the canvas show through, a technique often used by Mantegna. The earliest of these studies of the Virgin and Child is thought to be the one in Milan (Poldi Pezzoli). In its compostion it resembles the *Butler Madonna* (New York, Metropolitan Museum) and the painting of the same subject in Berlin (Staatliche Museen), though the latter is enclosed in a frame painted with six cherubs bearing the symbols of the Passion. The first of these is sometimes held to be a copy of a lost original, while the second seems to have been produced in collaboration with the Bellini workshop. But in both of them the vigorous spatial stress created by the figure of the infant Jesus, with his feet pointed outwards, would appear to be Mantegna's invention. The canvas in Milan still recalls the *Presentation in the Temple*, which we have already discussed. But in another *Madonna*, now in Bergamo (Accademia Carrara), the agile Christ Child appears again, and great emphasis is given to his kicking leg, the other leg being bent down and disappearing from view. It is difficult to establish a chronology for these paintings, especially because the Milan picture is smothered with thick yellow varnish. There is equal uncertainty about *The Christ Child Blessing* (Washington, National Gallery), for which many conflicting dates have been suggested.

Archival material suggests that in about 1478 Mantegna was active at the Marchese's residence at Bondanello, near Gonzaga, which has already been mentioned in connection with the *Meeting* scene in the *Camera degli Sposi* and where a 'grandiose palace' was in course of construction from 1468 onwards. In fact it was a reconstruction of an earlier building, and Mantegna was in charge of painting a frieze depicting the *Four Elements*. There is general agreement amongst most critics that the two engravings of the *Battle of the Sea Gods* may have some connection with this frieze, but we have no other evidence as to the appearance of the paintings in the palace at Bondanello, which was itself demolished in the eighteenth century. As for the engraving of the *Battle of the Sea Gods*, we are compelled to admire the urgency of the action and passions portrayed, dramatic despite the engraving technique, which crystalizes the outlines and splinters the surfaces and volumes, giving quite exceptional force to antique forms and bringing them to life.

*Battle of the Sea Gods
Engraving.*

The Roman Period

The first tribulations of advancing age, family troubles, the responsibility of surveying the work at the various residences of his patrons (who displayed a mania for building), and other duties connected with his service at court, left Mantegna little time to produce other works prior to his visit to Rome. His work as court artist was wide-ranging and onerous, and included, besides painting, the designing of miniatures, statues, tapestries, and precious objects, as well as two chests depicting the Justice of Trajan (Klagenfurt Museum) for the wedding of Paola Gonzaga to the Count of Gorizia in 1477. Above all, he was working on the series of canvasses depicting the *Triumph of Caesar*, which were already under way in 1486.

On 10 June 1488 Francesco II Gonzaga — who had succeeded as Marchese in 1484, on the death of his father Federico I who had himself succeeded Ludovico III in 1478 — wrote a letter of introduction to Pope Innocent VIII to present Maestro Andrea, then about to leave for Rome.

Before his departure the artist may have made the underdrawings, or *sinopie*, for the round paintings of the *Ascension* and *Saints Andrew and Longinus* (the latter dated 1488), which are certainly not by Mantegna but which created a considerable stir when they were discovered in about 1960 in the church of Sant'Andrea, Mantua, under some neo-classical frescoes that imitated their composition. If the fragmentary, badly preserved fresco of the head of St Andrew may possibly recall Mantegna's glowing colours and the solid solemnity of his forms, the mutilated fresco of the *Ascension*, arid and lifeless, is certainly to be rejected; it would even be optimistic to credit the master with the figure of Christ, though the design of this is repeated — in a far superior version — in an engraving certainly based on an autograph work. And it would be sheer defamation of character to ascribe to him — as has, alas, been done — the cherubs surrounding this figure, more wretched, if possible, than the fresco itself.

On 31 January 1489 Mantegna was in Rome, and wrote to the Marchese Gonzaga to remind him to take care of the parts of the *Triumph of Caesar* which were already finished. In another letter to the Marchese dated June 15th, the artist speaks of his work in progress, the decoration of a chapel in the Vatican, and complains that he barely earns enough to live on, while 'the work is great only to the man desirous of true honour, especially in Rome, where there are so many men who can judge wisely.' In the same letter there is a description of Djem, the brother of the Turkish sultan, whom the Pope was holding hostage. It is worth dwelling on because it conflicts with the idea of Mantegna as an austere, severe character which nineteenth century critics foisted on him. The artist is doubtless attempting to amuse the Marchese when he says that the prisoner displays 'a certain majestic pride', which however is somewhat undermined by a squint and an elephantine gait. Moreover his turban is made of 'thirty thousand rods' of material (almost 60,000 metres), and it appears that 'Bacchus visits him often.' He would like to paint him, but it is no easy matter, 'for now he has one look, and now another, like someone in love, so that I cannot hold his likeness in my mind.'

The Vatican chapel was demolished in the eighteenth century to make room for the papal archaeological museums. Old descriptions of it, which all agree on its small scale (it is often called 'cappellina' or 'cappelletta'), hint at 'pleasing' views of towns and villages, 'simulated marbles' and 'painted divisions, round in form, woven together in the manner of a grating' in the 'little cupola'; while the ceiling of an adjacent sacresty displays 'attractive views framed in squares, circles and eight-sided figures', 'festoons of fruit', *Chiaroscuri* with gold backgrounds', 'heads of cherubs scattered here and there', allegories of 'heroic virtues', and 'putti holding up an oval' containing the dedication and the date: 1490. All this was the framework for frescoed episodes from the life of John the Baptist (*The Baptism of Christ*, *The Dance of Salome*, the *Beheading*

of the *Baptist* etc.), which were enlivened by torturers, guards, bystanders, 'banquets in a real garden', 'crowds of the faithful', and angels. And there were other scenes (*The Nativity, Epiphany* etc.), single figures of saints and evangelists, and the portrait of Pope Innocent VIII who had commissioned the work. In short, it incorporated much of the decorative repertoire developed in the *Camera degli Sposi*, but adapted to a sacred theme and painted with Mantegna's fastidious care, so that Vasari could write that the walls seemed more like miniatures than frescoes.

Vasari also assigns to the Roman period the *Madonna of the Stonecutters*, now in the Uffizi. This has been seen as an allegory of redemption because the landscape to the right of the Christ Child is immersed in shadow, with masons working on the column and the sarcophagus, attributes of the Passion; while on the other side the fields are gold with grain, the shepherds lead their flocks, and a city glitters in the sun, all symbols of Christianity. Mantegna has painted the rocks and slabs of stone in extraordinary detail, almost like a geological study, and realistically conveys the harshness and hardness of the material; the incredible outcrop of shaly stone is struck by the reflected rays of the sunset, and the clear green light of the sky is diffused over the whole scene, blurring the outlines of the distant hill and of the gigantic overhanging cliff.

The recurrence of quarry-workers and sunset — here painted in livid tones of yellows and pale blues — has led the majority of critics to place the Copenhagen *Pietà* (Statens Museum) in the Roman period. Certainly the pictorial idiom, as well as the perspective and composition, which with Mantegna constitute a prime factor in dating his works, are close to those of the *Madonna of the Stonecutters*, so that such a connection does seem plausible. However, a different emotional tone has been discerned in the Copenhagen *Pietà*: the narration of the story, which in earlier works has been understated and self-contained, is now expressed violently and becomes 'an affirmation of energy, shrieked out almost bitterly, in which grief is expressed in a continual contraction of outlines' (Cipriani, 1956).

This new expression of grief is also apparent in the *Dead Christ* in the Brera (Milan), although it does not necessarily belong to the Roman period and has been variously dated from the end of the Padua period (about 1457) to 1500 and even later. We need hardly mention the fame of the perspectival construction of this picture, painted in such a way that the image of the Redeemer 'follows' the observer around the room, using an illusionistic technique similar to that employed for the oculus in the ceiling of the *Camera degli Sposi* but in this case so overwhelming as to eclipse every other expressive element. Modern critics are rather thrown out by this work, and vagueness about the date — a span of nearly half a century — is matched by an equal disagreement about its artistic value, which should not be confined exclusively to an appreciation of the foreshortened viewpoint. The eerie lighting of the painting has been described as a 'livid twilight.' There are those who think the figures of the two mourners are later additons, as if to explain the lack

(previous page)
Pietà
1489-90. 83x51 cm.
Copenhagen, Statens Museum.

Madonna of the Stonecutters
1489-90. 29x21,5 cm.
Florence, Uffizi.

Dead Christ
1490. 66x81 cm.
Milan, Brera.

of coherence with the rest of the composition so often commented on (Marangoni, 1933). In fact a 'Cristo in scurto' is mentioned among the works still in the artist's studio at the time of his death in 1506, which may or may not be this one: it was bought shortly after Mantegna's death by Sigismondo Gonzaga, the little boy in the *Meeting* of the *Camera degli Sposi*, who had since become a cardinal. But can it be identified with the Milan picture? That the latter is genuine has never been doubted, but it is equally true that clues gleaned from the archives would seem to indicate that there were two versions of the *Dead Christ*. The Glen Head version, in a New York private collection, does not help us to fill the gap in spite of the accolade bestowed by some experts, since it is a modest copy dating from the end of the sixteenth century or even later. But it does diverge in several details from the Milan painting and does not

include the two mourners, so that if we take it to be an exact copy, it must imply the former existence of another original. This, together with the fact that the conditon of the Brera painting is very poor (due partly to extensive repainting, which is unlikely to have been done by Mantegna himself), suggest that we ought to suspend judgement on the matter.

On 16 December 1489 Francesco II Gonzaga, who was about to marry Isabella d'Este, wrote to the pope requesting him to authorize Mantegna's return to Mantua to help with the preparations for this wedding. From the pope's reply (1 January 1490) we learn that Mantegna was ill, and that it would be dangerous to expose 'such a man' to the discomforts of a journey. Also, the Vatican chapel can not have been finished, since it was only dated in that year. His return to Mantua, therefore, took place in September or early October of 1490.

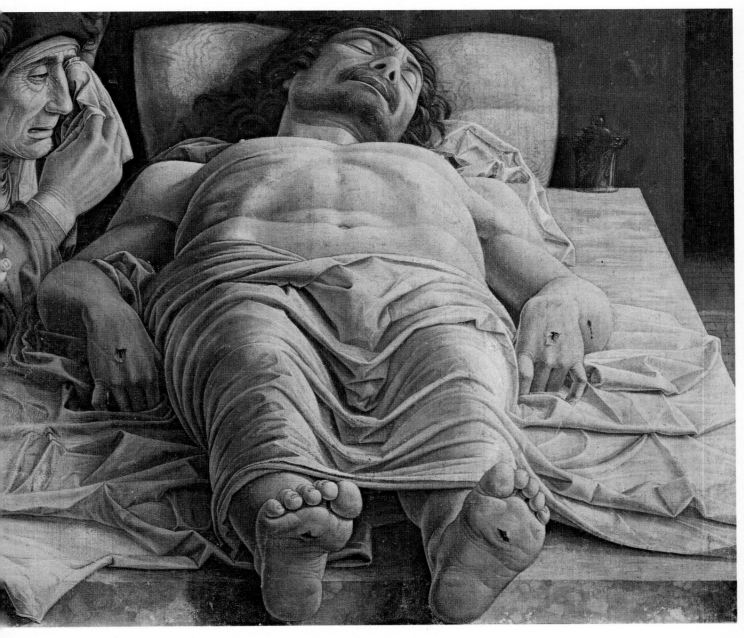

The Triumph of Caesar

Mantēgna had worked on and off in the Marchese's residence at Marmirolo since April 1481, and there, between 1491 and 1494, various painters worked under his supervision on four rooms known respectively as the 'Room of the Horses', the 'Room of the Map of the World', the 'Room of the Cities', and the 'Greek Room.' This last room was painted with views of Constantinople, Gallipoli, Hadrianopolis, Rhodes and other Levantine places, showing interiors of mosques, bath-houses and other typically Turkish subjects — further proof of Mantegna's endless invention. In the same palace there was also a series of *Triumphs* based on the description of a triumphant procession by Petrarch, a theme to which he returned in 1501 for the scenery for a theatrical performance in Mantua. Unfortunately, like the castles of Cavriana, Goito and Bondanello, that at Marmirolo has been demolished.

In February 1492 Marchese Francesco gave Mantegna a piece of woodland in reward for his work on the chapel in the Castel San Giorgio (probably the paintings connected with the Uffizi triptych), the *Camera degli Sposi*, and the *Triumph of Caesar*.

The Triumph of Caesar consists of nine large canvasses (274 x 274 cm), certainly begun by 1486, still incomplete six years later (at the time of the donation of the wood), and in fact never completed, for in a letter of 1494 the cycle is said to be lacking two pieces, which were never painted. We know that in 1497 Bishop Ludovico Gonzaga thought of using the canvasses to decorate a courtyard, but possibly the perishable nature of the tempera in which they are painted discouraged him from exposing them to the open air. They were used, together with the *Triumphs* based on Petrarch, in the theatrical performance of 1501, but we do not know in what capacity or how they were arranged. On the death of the artist in 1506 the nine canvasses were still in the house he had built at Porta Pusterla, near the church of St Sebastian, on a piece of land granted him by Marchese Ludovico; but this evidently remained the property of the Gonzagas, as did the house and the series of *Triumphs*, for in the early seventeenth century the paintings were taken back to the palace, where they were copied by Rubens. Shortly afterwards they were sold to Charles I of England, after two years of haggling (1627 to 1629), and carried out of the country secretly because the paintings were so popular that it was feared their sale might cause riots. This popularity is demonstrated by the fact that people began to copy them as early as 1492 or 1493. Today the great canvasses are in the Orangery of Hampton Court Palace; recently they have been cleaned of all later additions (apart from one canvas, that of the *Captives*, which was in too bad a state to be restored).

For obvious reasons the cycle was compared to classical reliefs and associated with Mantegna's stay in Rome (though modern critics exclude the possibility that his Roman sojourn influenced the iconography of the series); the *Triumphs* have also been linked with the triumphal processions that in the Middle Ages and the Renaissance took place on many occasions: princely weddings and funerals, carnivals and grand receptions; and with literary sources, particularly the *De re militari* of Valturio (published in Verona, 1472) and even more the *Romaika* (History of Rome) by Appian of Alexandria (2nd century A.D.), partly because Mantegna shows a certain preference for Greek texts. The iconological meaning of the series has given rise to some complex hypotheses. According to one thesis the antique motifs — festoons, animals' skulls etc. — are symbols or pictographic characters, each with a precise meaning, and formulated by Mantegna using the same system that L.B. Alberti believed to have been adopted by the Romans in respect of Egyptian hieroglyphics. The *Triumph* should therefore be seen as a 'dream' with no exact classical references.

Even the fact that the paintings were hung in the house at Porta Pusterla immediately after Manteg-

*The Triumph of Caesar.
The series consists of nine
canvasses of identical
dimensions. (274x274 cm.)
The cycle was begun by
1486; in 1494 it was still
incomplete, as a letter states
that two panels were still
missing, but these were
never painted.*

*This page, two canvasses:
The Picture Bearers.
The Triumphal Car.
Hampton Court Palace.*

na's death has given rise to a number of hypotheses. The nine canvasses were placed round the circular courtyard, which had four porticoes, in the spaces between the pilasters. Thus for anyone standing in the centre of the courtyard the pilasters covered the breaks between the canvasses, creating the effect of a single uninterrupted composition, as Mantegna may have originally intended. Further proof of the relationship between the paintings and the architecture of the building can be deduced from an engraving by one of Mantegna's followers, in which

The Litter Bearers.
Hampton Court Palace.

the canvas of the trophy-bearers is flanked by a pilaster which conceals part of an elephant, the body of which is continued on the next canvas where it and others of its kind are seen accompanying the sacrificial bulls. Obviously the column is super-imposed over the animal. All the same there is no confirmation of any continuous arrangement of all nine canvasses, either in a circle or in a horizontal row.

Indeed, if we take what is presumed to be the first canvas of the series, Julius Caesar on his

The Vase Bearer.
Hampton Court Palace.

triumphal chariot, this is shown with its side parallel to the picture's surface, while the very next canvas, which includes the back of the chariot, is viewed at an angle. The same discrepancies are apparent in the other panels: in one the vanishing point is just below the centre, in another it is shifted to the right-hand side, and in a third canvas it is lowered; while because of the variable angle from which they are viewed 'sotto-in-su' the figures sometimes appear to be in the foreground and in other cases sufficiently far back for their feet to be hidden. In short the

The Elephants.
Hampton Court Palace.

perspective changes constantly, and forces the observer to make corresponding adjustments. Each panel has a single viewpoint, but the sequence of nine canvasses creates a multiple perspective, or rather presupposes that the audience will move about, a system anticipated in the work of Paolo Uccello. What does not vary is Mantegna's assiduous adherence to truth; and, along with this, his attempt to attain coherence of atmosphere rather than of composition, in which the pictorial language is firmer than ever in defining details and violent

The Corselet Bearers.
Hampton Court Palace.

The Captives.
Hampton Court Palace.

The Musicians.
Hampton Court Palace.

foreshortenings, but also in effecting skilful changes of scale, and creates a rigorously unified harmony. For this reason the clamour created by the wealth of figures ends in a feeling of tranquility close to that of the *Camera degli Sposi* in Mantua, and no less convincing and immediate to us.

(following page)
Detail of
The Picture
Bearers.

Caesar on his Chariot.
Hampton Court Palace.

The Late Works

One of the reasons why the Milan *Dead Christ* has been placed among the last works of Mantegna is its dark subject matter of death, since it is often supposed that artists, particularly great ones, are aware of their approaching end.

For similar reasons, the *St Sebastian* in the Ca'd'Oro, Venice, is often given a late dating, since the scroll entwined around the candle in the righthand foreground states in Latin as bitter as it is transparent: 'Nihil nisi divinum stabile est. Coetera fumus' ('Only the divine is stable. The rest is smoke'). Like the Brera canvas, the *St Sebastian* was on the list of works still in the artist's studio when he died, and it seems to have been destined for Bishop Ludovico Gonzaga. Its later changes of ownership have been exhaustively documented. The general opinion that it dates from shortly before his death is challenged by only a couple of critics, who place it nearer the *Triumph of Caesar*, and to judge from the painted framework, we might well think it could be dated around the beginning of that series. The condition of the painting might explain why it was still in the studio after so many years, for it shows signs of a total reworking (which must be by Mantegna himself, either because he was dissatisfied with the original version, or for some other reason), as well as the addition of a loin cloth, no doubt because the sight of pubic hair would have shocked Monsignor Ludovico. This additon to the drapery is so obvious that we are forced to wonder how it has escaped the notice of so many students, for this clumsy mess of white lead paint is formless and totally out of keeping with the precision and rhythmic elegance of the original painting. It must be the work of an assistant, possibly Francesco, Mantegna's son, who followed his father's profession on a modest level. Whatever the case, it does not silence the cry from the figure of the martyr, who bursts out from the space inside the painted 'window', tormented by the arrows which have wounded him from every side.

The canvas of *Christ the Redeemer* at Correggio (Congregazione della Carità), which is possibly a fragment of a larger work and in bad condition, certainly belongs to 1493, for it is signed and dated. Close to it in style is the *Holy Family with the Baptist and a Saint* in Dresden (Gemäldegalerie) which, in its static serenity, reminds us of another composition known in two different versions. These focus on the figure of the Child, flanked by the infant Baptist, with the Virgin painted below them in the act of sewing. In the Paris version (Petit Palais), Jesus and the infant Baptist are leaning on a sill, and the picture also contains the head of a saint; in the London version (National Gallery) there is the head of St Joseph, and the parapet has been transformed into a well, which rather oddly (and incongruously, unless it is intended to be the mystical well of the *hortus conclusus*) encloses the figure of the Virgin sewing. Neither of the two versions seems genuine, but presumably they both derive from a lost original or drawing, and they show that Mantegna's inventiveness was still very much alive.

So we come to the *Madonna of Victory* (Louvre), commissioned by Francesco II Gonzaga, who is seen kneeling on the left, being blessed by the Virgin, and accompanied by St Michael and St Andrew. These are balanced on the other side by St Longinus and St George (with the broken lance, as in the small painting of St George in the Venice Accademia), and by a kneeling female figure identified either as St Elizabeth, because she is beside the Baptist, or St Anne, or Isabella d'Este the Wife of Francesco (though she has a halo), or even a certain Osanna, a contemporary Mantuan woman with a saintly reputation. The branch of coral hanging above is not simply a good luck charm, but had the power of warding off 'fiendish monsters.'

The commission for this painting is connected with an episode sadly not uncommon, and by no means edifying. In 1493 a certain Daniele de Norsa, a Jew, had bought a house in Mantua where there was a fresco depicting the *Madonna and Saints*. After obtaining permission from the ecclesiastical author-

St Sebastian
1490. 210x91 cm.
Venice, Ca' d'Oro.
The inscription reads 'Nihil
nisi divinum stabile est.
Coetera fumus'.

ities, the new proprietor had this removed; this provoked riots, and the upshot was that the Jew was fined a hundred and ten ducats. This sum was paid to Mantegna as emolument for the *Madonna of Victory*, which was to be placed in the Cappella della Vittoria, built as an ex-voto for the Marchese's surprisingly lucky victory over the French at Fornovo on 6 July 1495. On the first anniversary of the battle the altarpiece was solemnly installed in its chapel, amid scenes of indescribable jubilation. Nineteenth century critics were less enthusiastic about this work, pointing out the lack of proportion in the composition and the general hardness of tone; and more recent scholars have criticized the painting for attempting to reconcile rigid symmetries and asymmetries, for the disparity between the pearly lighting and the dazzling splendour of the fruit and the parrots on the pergola, and the inconsistency between the vast scale of the picture (280 x 160 cm) and the miniaturistic exactitude of the technique.

In fact this is a work torn from its original context. The chapel no longer exists, but presumably the painting was stylistically suited to its setting, especially if (as Vasari states, although this has been denied by nineteenth century scholars) Mantegna himself designed the Cappella della Vittoria, as he certainly designed the frame of the altarpiece (also lost). We notice in this painting an echo of the San Zeno polyptych in the abandonment of the 'scenic' perspective to which the artist had remained faithful ever since the Ovetari frescoes. This change was already evident in the Dresden canvas of the *Holy Family with the Baptist and a Saint*, and before that in the *Madonna of the Stonecutters*. Or rather, after his early rejection of the official perspective of Brunelleschi, and the adoption of the 'anti-classical' system of Donatello, Mantegna in later life formulated his own concept, derived from Brunelleschi, of space as an ideal measure of the world, and identified art with a higher form of harmony, just when Botticelli and Michelangelo were beginning to subvert this ideal. This is why in the *Madonna of Victory* the *trompe-l'oeil* effects are perfectly judged, and there is the dramatic intensification created by the *sotto-in-su* viewpoint, as in the *Triumph of Caesar*; once again the action is unified by the atmospheric chromatic treatment, accentuated by the richness of the colours, which is used to emphasise the figure of the Marchese (who commissioned the picture) by means of a bold counterpoint of light and shadow. But these devices are no longer used to obtain absolute fidelity to the visible world, but instead to create an abstract, intellectualized vision.

Christ the Redeemer
1493. 53x43 cm.
Correggio, Congregazione
di Carità. This is probably
a fragment of a larger
work.

Holy Family with the
Baptist and a Saint
c 1493. 75,5x61,5 cm.
Dresden, Staatliche
Gemäldegalerie.

Holy Family (Imperator
Mundi)
Paris, Petit Palais.
This painting, together
with the version in the
National Gallery, London,
is almost certainly a copy
of a lost original.

Trivulzio Madonna
1497. 287x214 cm.
Milan, Castello Sforzesco.
On the left is St John the
Baptist; the other saints are
probably Gregory,
Benedict and Jerome.

Madonna and Child with
Saints
c 1495. 61,5x87,5 cm.
Turin, Galleria Sabauda.
It is difficult to identify
the saints with the
exception of the Baptist
and St Catherine of
Alexandria, to the right
with the wheel.

In the ducal palace in Mantua there is a drawing, made with a brush and white lead on dark paper, of exactly the same size as the altarpiece of the *Madonna of Victory*, although a strip about 15 centimetres broad has been removed from the bottom. Scholars have considered it a genuine cartoon by Mantegna, though it shows no signs of having been used as such and is therefore thought to have been made expressly to be shown to the Marchese for his approval, who was at that time in Venice. Others hold that it is a tracing taken from the altarpiece before this was carried off to France, along with the rest of Napoleon's booty. This seems the more likely hypothesis.

The *Trivulzio Madonna* (Milan, Castello Sforzesco) is inscribed with the date 15 August 1497; in it the Baptist is immediately recognisable, and the other saints are probably Saints Gregory the Great, Benedict and Jerome. It was painted for the high altar of the church of Santa Maria in Organo in Verona, a model of which is shown in the hands of St Jerome. The French critic Bazin, who must be taken seriously, described it in 1961 as 'curiously unsuccessful', an opinion at variance with the majority of critics who admire the painting, particularly for its exclusion of any reference to real space, an effect achieved by taking a very low viewpoint. Thanks to this choice of viewpoint the vertical movement of the composition as a whole, aided by the chromatic brilliance of the 'wings' of the painting, has been said to take on 'the resonance of an immense nave.' In fact this interpretation is hard to accept, for the perspective is even further removed from the Donatello type than in the Victory altarpiece. Mantegna has adopted a format of classical composure: the oval of the Virgin's face — although it has a certain chromatic decorativeness previously foreign to Mantegna — becomes the centre of a series of waves radiating from the almond-shaped aureole, containing the cherubs, to its outer reflection composed of foliage and saints. The layout does not attempt to be realistic but is based on an *a priori* concept, and the only reminder of earlier experiments is the tension created between the *sotto-in-sù* viewpoint of the four saints and the contrasted foreshortening of the angel-musicians at the bottom. It is hard to establish whether the rigidly frontal presentation of the central group aims at stressing this tension or, as seems more probable, at mitigating it.

The year 1497 is also the year of the *Parnassus*, the first of the paintings made for the *Studiolo* of the Marchesa Isabella d'Este in the Castel San Giorgio. This lady's notion to create a 'thinking-room', decorated with mythological paintings by the greatest contemporary artists, dates from about two years earlier and must have been based on a precisely worked out programme, although this has been denied. Nevertheless, of the various painters concerned in the project, Perugino in 1503 signed a contract in which the subject-matter was laid down in the minutest detail, while Giovanni Bellini, asked to contribute a painting in 1501, struggled in vain to ensure himself complete freedom, and finally abandoned the project.

One of the rooms in the palace in Mantua now contains the original frames for these paintings, for which Mantegna issued specific instructions; but this is not their original home, as the *Studiolo* was shifted several times to various parts of the castle.

Pegasus, the winged horse, and Mercury. Detail of the right hand side of Parnassus.
According to tradition the song of the Muses caused volcanic eruptions and other catastrophes, which were only stopped when Pegasus stamped his hoof on the ground.

Parnassus
1497. 160x192 cm.
Paris, Louvre.
The first of the paintings commissioned by Isabella d'Este for her Studiolo in the castle of San Giorgio.

We are certain, however, that the series included three paintings by Mantegna, Perugino's *Contest Between Love and Chastity*, and an allegory by Lorenzo Costa. And we know that these five canvasses, together with two others by Correggio and a lost pair by Mantegna which decorated the doorway opposite the entrance, were still in Isabella's apartments after her death. In 1605 they were moved to the *Appartamento del Paradiso*; then in about 1627 they became the property of Cardinal Richelieu, and thereafter of Louis XIV, until in 1801 they were sent to the Louvre, where they still are.

The *Parnassus* poses a number of iconographical problems. The dancing Muses are easily identified, both on account of their number and the presence of the crumbling mountains in the top left hand corner: for there was a tradition that the song of the nine sisters caused volcanic eruptions and similar cataclysms, which were only terminated by Pegasus stamping his hoof on the ground — and indeed we see the winged horse on the right, ready to do just that. Beside him is Mercury, whose presence is justified by the protection which he (and Apollo)

afforded the adulteress in the love affair between Mars and Venus, which is the real subject of the picture. The two lovers are seen standing on the peak of Parnassus, beside a bed. The betrayed husband, Vulcan, appears on the left, at the entrance to his forge; he is identified by his blacksmith's implements, and is looking towards the faithless pair. Apollo is seated lower down, his lyre in his hands. It seems unnecessary to identify this figure as Orpheus, although it so appears in a 1542 inventory of the palace of Mantua, despite the fact that Phoe-

'Otium' and 'Inertia'.
Detail of the lower part of
the Triumph of Virtue
(Minerva Expels the Vices).

bus Apollo is quite normally shown among the Muses. From what we read in the contract made with Perugino, and from what we see in the other paintings of the series, there can be no doubt about the didactic intention of the work as a whole. So much so, indeed, that it might seem obvious to read the *Parnassus* as a condemnation by the Muses of the illicit union of Mars and Venus. Nevertheless, it appears that the learned men of the court did not disapprove of the affair, and this gave rise to the complicated interpretation of the *Parnassus* as an erotic burlesque suggested by Wind in 1949, and rejected by later scholars. Technically the painting anticipates the colouring typical of Venetian painting in the early sixteenth century, and even the Olympian harmony achieved by Raphael only after 1510. It has also been pointed out that there are echoes of the goddess rising from the waves, painted years earlier by Botticelli in the *Birth of Venus*.

Undoubtedly Mantegna shows certain traits, already in part discernible in the *Trivulzio Madonna*, that differentiate him from his predecessors: there is a greater concern in fusing all the elements of the composition — landscapes and figures, mountains that echo the shape of deliberately unusual gestures — and more attention is paid to the careful balancing of masses and spaces, the tightening of forms and the gathering together of all the main lines of the composition. To take a single instance, in the *Parnassus*, the Muse who turns to Apollo bends towards him with a kind of uncomfortable naturalness, in order to repeat the line of the hillock that acts as Mars' and Venus's bedchamber.

The Triumph of Virtue
c 1504. 160x192 cm.
Paris, Louvre.

Minerva, detail from the
Triumph of Virtue.

Apart from making use of Brunelleschi's theory of perspective, Mantegna — and this was a genuine discovery, in which he was preceded only by Leonardo — was reaching towards a supreme harmony that transformed the vision of the world into ideal beauty: in a word, towards the fully-fledged classical spirit of the high Renaissance, the culmination of Brunelleschi's original concept.

The *Triumph of Virtue* was completed in 1502 as a companion-piece to the *Parnassus*. Minerva, the virtuous goddess, is seen expelling the shameless Venus along with the Vices from the Garden of Virtue, as we learn from the scroll wrapped around the Mother of Virtue (to the left), who is imprisoned in an olive tree. From the sky the Cardinal Virtues look down with satisfaction, though it is not clear why the rocks in the background are crumbling into the shapes of monsters, and the clouds are taking on human features. The literary sources have been identified as the *Dream of Poliphylus* (Venice, 1472)

and the *De genealogia deorum gentilium* of Boccacio. Beneath a sky that is the most impressive in European art before Altdorfer, and surrounded by enjoyable fantasies (the goddess-cum-olive tree is worthy of Bosch at his best), the progress of Minerva is impeded by the swarm of Vices, who themselves are held up by Venus, intent on tidying herself up a bit before being forced to flee; while on the right hand side the group of Inertia and an ape carrying Sloth is uncomfortably foreshortened, in order that it should fit into the triangular construction which Mantegna had so rigidly imposed upon the composition.

The third canvas painted for the *Studiolo* is the *Myth of the God Comus*, started by Mantegna but completed after his death by Lorenzo Costa, who evidently touched up the parts already done and thus made it impossible to distinguish Mantegna's hand.

74

Holy Family with St John the Baptist and his Parents c. 1505. 40x169 cm. Mantua, Church of Sant'Andrea, Mantegna's Funerary Chapel.

Baptism of Christ c 1505. 228x175 cm. Mantua, Church of Sant'Andrea, Mantegna's Funerary Chapel.

Also dating from the master's last years are the canvasses done for his funerary chapel in the church of Sant'Andrea in Mantua, depicting the *Holy Family with St John the Baptist and his Parents* and the *Baptism of Christ*, and painted largely with the help of assistants amongst whom some scholars number Correggio, then not much more than fifteen years old. The same chapel contains the bronze bust of the artist, which is generally held to be a self-portrait, and which he may have made·between 1480 and 1490. Of the many pieces of sculpture attributed to him over the years, this is the only one that undoubtedly comes from his hand.

To return to Isabella's *Studiolo*, our examination would be incomplete without a postscript defining the part played by the artist in the conception of these works. The canvasses should really be seen as the work of a team of three: the Marchesa who commissioned them, and whose relations with Mantegna had been stormy since at least 1493; the author of the literary programme (who may have been Paride Ceresara), bent on including every possible allegorical detail; and Mantegna himself, accepting orders from the other two, and attempting to interpret them in paint, ultimately to the detriment of his art.

In terms of the history of art, however, the responsibility for this late style is finally his. Approaching old age is not a sufficient explanation for the crisis in his art that had made him turn to classical sources for inspiration as early as 1490, when he was less than sixty. This crisis quite clearly arose from the desire to find new forms of expression, and — although the results were utterly personal — was perhaps stimulated by Leonardo's presence in Milan, which had links with Mantua because of the relations between the Gonzagas and the Sforzas.

Occasio et Poenitentia
c 1495. 168x146 cm.
Mantua, Ducal Palace.

Samson and Delilah
c 1495. 47x37 cm.
London, National Gallery.
On the tree is written:
'Foemina diabolo tribus
assibus est mala peior'.

This obsessive classicism is also evident in another group of works, often neglected, which date from the same time as the *Studiolo* and in which Mantegna achieves a convincing and coherent style. These are monochrome paintings, all simulating marble bas-reliefs, sometimes applied to a coloured stone background and obviously drawing on his geological expertise. We know of no precedents for these pictures in 'portable' painting (though similar grisailles abound in mural decoration), and the whole *genre* probably first started with the *Judith* (Dublin, National Gallery), which is partly executed by assistants. The work of assistants is even more apparent in the pair of paintings of *Judith* and *Dido* in Montreal (Art Association) and in the *Mucius Scaevola* in Munich (Graphische Sammlung); it is preponderant in the *Sacrifice of Isaac* in Vienna (Kunsthistorisches Museum), and practically smothers Mantegna's invention in the *Occasio et Poenitentia* in Mantua (Ducal Palace). However the *Samson and Delilah* (London, National Gallery) is brilliantly inventive and obviously by Mantegna himself, and three further paintings in the same gallery, the *Introduction of the Cult of Cybele to Rome*, a *Tuccia* and a *Sophonisba*, are painted with spectacular virtuosity.

The theme of the largest of these, the *Introduction of the Cult of Cybele to Rome*, is an episode from the Second Punic War. When Hannibal had landed in Italy the Sybilline Books demanded that the bust of the Mother of the Gods, Cybele, should be transferred from Pergamon to Rome in order to protect the city from invasion. In addition, the Delphic Oracle had decreed that the image should be received by the most worthy of the Romans, and the senate selected Publius Cornelius Scipio Nasica for this honour: the painting was in fact commissioned by the Venetian Francesco Cornaro,

Introduction of the Cult of
Cybele to Rome
1505-06. 73,5x268 cm.
London, National Gallery.

whose family claimed descent from Scipio, hence the subject matter. Through this story involving his remote ancestors, Cornaro evidently wished to exalt feminine chastity, as we may infer from the two other paintings which he commissioned at the same time: that of the Vestal Virgin Tuccia (who, in order to prove her innocence of incest succeeded in carrying water in a sieve from the Tiber to her own temple) and that of Queen Sophonisba (who poisoned herself rather than fall into the hands of the Romans when they defeated her husband Masinissa); while a central character in the Cybele canvas is the matron Claudia Quinta, who, as the bust entered Rome, succeeded in proving her own virtue, on which doubt had been shed. The three works, probably commissioned by March 1505, were not finished in the following January. The master succeeded in completing them before he died on 13 September 1506 (a few touches by other hands can be discerned only in the *Tuccia* and the *Sophonisba*), and his heirs returned some unused material to Cornaro.

Thus Mantegna's final artistic statement is to be found in the Cornaro group of paintings, imbued with the spirit of classicism, yet filled with life and not dry, pedantic archaeological exercises. In these last works he has achieved a perfect formal equilibrium in which every mutable feature in the composition is fixed, made abstract and eternal. Yet the rhetoric of these 'sacred marbles' is dissolved in the expression of anguish which restores dramatic life to conventional forms, an anguish which was shared by his Florentine contemporary Botticelli (although he expressed it through Gothic anti-realism, a style utterly foreign to Mantegna), and which was to reappear in the work of the Mannerist painters.

Sophonisba
1505-06. 72,5x23 cm.
London, National Gallery.

Tuccia
1505-06. 72,5x23 cm.
London, National Gallery.

Self-portrait
1480-90
Mantua, church of
Sant'Andrea, Mantegna's
Funerary Chapel.

Selected Bibliography

P. Kristeller, *Andrea Mantegna,* London 1901

E. Tietze-Conrat, *Mantegna,* London 1955

G. Fiocco, *L'arte di Andrea Mantegna,* 2nd edition Venice 1959

R. Cipriani, *Tutta la pittura di Andrea Mantegna,* Milan 1956

L. Coletti and E. Camesasca, *La Camera degli Sposi del Mantegna,* Milan 1959

G. Paccagnini and A. Mezzetti, *Andrea Mantegna* (exhibition catalogue), Venice 1961

E. Camesasca, *Andrea Mantegna,* Milan 1964

A.M. Romanini, *L'itinerario pittorico del Mantegna,* Milan 1966